Lady Penelope Devereux: Sir Philip Sidney's Muse

A Tudor Times Insight

By Tudor Times

Published by Tudor Times Ltd

Tudor Times Insights

Tudor Times Insights are books collating articles from our website www.tudortimes.co.uk which is a repository for a wide variety of information about the Tudor and Stewart period 1485 – 1625. There you can find material on People, Places, Daily Life, Military & Warfare, Politics & Economics and Religion. The site has a Book Review section, with author interviews and a book club. It also features comprehensive family trees, and a 'What's On' event list with information about forthcoming activities relevant to the Tudors and Stewarts.

Titles in the Series

Profiles

Katherine Parr: Henry VIII's Sixth Queen

James IV: King of Scots

Lady Margaret Pole: Countess of Salisbury

Thomas Wolsey: Henry VIII's Cardinal

Marie of Guise: Regent of Scotland

Thomas Cromwell: Henry VIII's Chief Minister

Lady Penelope Devereux: Sir Philip Sidney's Muse

James V: Scotland's Renaissance King

Lady Katherine Grey: Tudor Prisoner

Sir William Cecil: Elizabeth I's Chief Minister

Lady Margaret Douglas: Countess of Lennox

Sir James Melville: Scottish Ambassador

Tudors & Stewarts 2015: A collection fo 12 Profiles

People

Who's Who in Wolf Hall

Politics & Economy

Field of Cloth of Gold

Succession: The Tudor Problem

The Pilgrimage of Grace and Exeter Conspiracy

Contents

Introduction 6

Family Tree...7

Lady Penelope Devereux' Life Story 8

Aspects of Lady Penelope Devereux' Life 23

Bibliography...38

Lady Penelope Devereux: Sir Philip Sidney's Muse

Introduction

Penelope Devereux was one of the leading lights of the late Elizabethan and early Stuart courts. Her beauty and charm, coupled with her intelligence and education, led her to be the centre of the circle of soldiers and patrons of art around her brother, the Earl of Essex. Like Essex, however, she was impetuous and single-minded and could not resist flirting with intrigue and danger.

Penelope led the life of a great lady, travelling extensively between the homes of both her family of origin and her those of her husband, as well as attending court in and around London.

In an age when even aristocratic women, once they were married, tended to be confined to hearth and home, Penelope led a life of excitement and novelty. Far from the docile, submissive wife that was the Elizabethan ideal, Penelope was a force to be reckoned with.

Part 7 contains Lady Penelope Devereux's Life Story and additional articles about her, looking at different aspects of her life.

Family Tree

Penelope DEVEREUX
Lady Penelope Rich

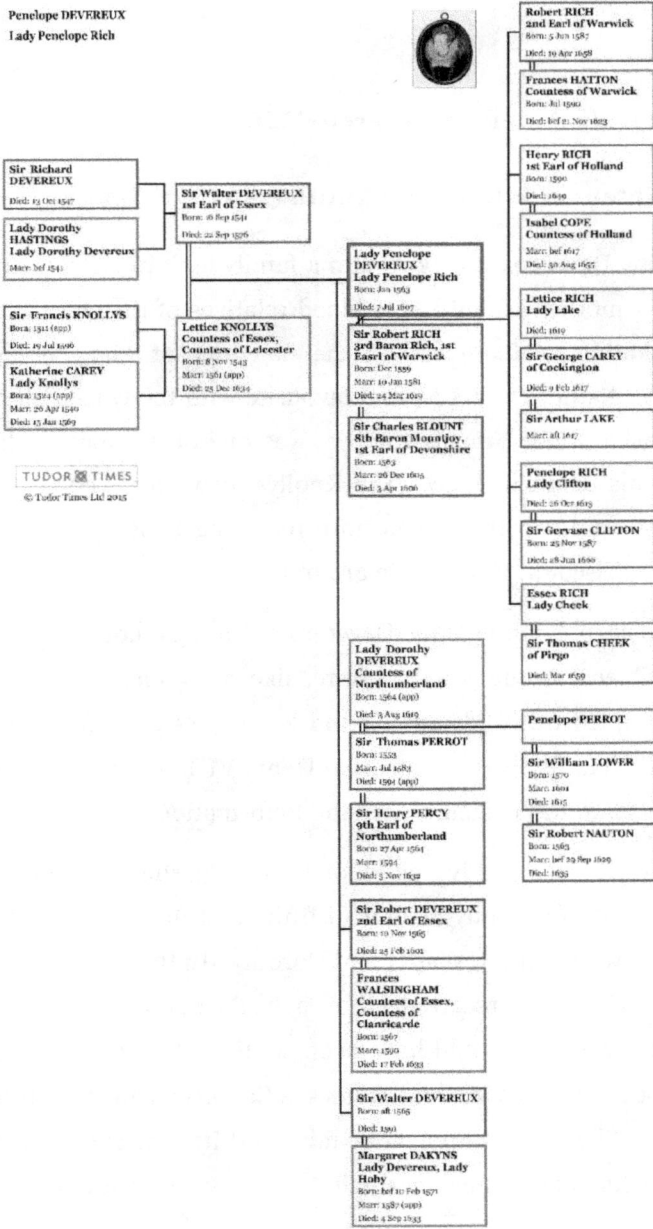

Robert RICH
2nd Earl of Warwick
Born: 5 Jun 1587
Died: 19 Apr 1658

Frances HATTON
Countess of Warwick
Born: Jul 1590
Died: bef 2: Nov 1623

Henry RICH
1st Earl of Holland
Born: 1590
Died: 1649

Isabel COPE
Countess of Holland
Marr: bef 1617
Died: 30 Aug 1655

Sir Richard DEVEREUX
Died: 13 Oct 1547

Lady Dorothy HASTINGS
Lady Dorothy Devereux
Marr: bef 1541

Sir Walter DEVEREUX
1st Earl of Essex
Born: 16 Sep 1541
Died: 22 Sep 1576

Lady Penelope DEVEREUX
Lady Penelope Rich
Born: Jan 1563
Died: 7 Jul 1607

Lettice RICH
Lady Lake
Died: 1619

Sir Francis KNOLLYS
Born: 1511 (app.)
Died: 19 Jul 1596

Katherine CAREY
Lady Knollys
Born: 1524 (app.)
Marr: 26 Apr 1540
Died: 15 Jan 1569

Lettice KNOLLYS
Countess of Essex,
Countess of Leicester
Born: 8 Nov 1543
Marr: 1561 (app.)
Died: 25 Dec 1634

Sir Robert RICH
3rd Baron Rich, 1st
Earl of Warwick
Born: Dec 1559
Marr: 10 Jan 1581
Died: 24 Mar 1619

Sir George CAREY
of Cockington
Died: 9 Feb 1617

Sir Charles BLOUNT
8th Baron Mountjoy,
1st Earl of Devonshire
Born: 1563
Marr: 26 Dec 1605
Died: 3 Apr 1606

Sir Arthur LAKE
Marr: aft 1617

Penelope RICH
Lady Clifton
Died: 26 Oct 1613

Sir Gervase CLIFTON
Born: 25 Nov 1587
Died: 28 Jun 1660

Essex RICH
Lady Cheek

Sir Thomas CHEEK
of Pirgo
Died: Mar 1659

Lady Dorothy DEVEREUX
Countess of Northumberland
Born: 1564 (app.)
Died: 3 Aug 1619

Penelope PERROT

Sir Thomas PERROT
Born: 1553
Marr: Jul 1583
Died: 1594 (app.)

Sir William LOWER
Born: 1570
Marr: 1601
Died: 1615

Sir Henry PERCY
9th Earl of Northumberland
Born: 27 Apr 1564
Marr: 1594
Died: 5 Nov 1632

Sir Robert NAUTON
Born: 1563
Marr: bef 29 Sep 1609
Died: 1635

Sir Robert DEVEREUX
2nd Earl of Essex
Born: 10 Nov 1565
Died: 25 Feb 1601

Frances WALSINGHAM
Countess of Essex,
Countess of Clanricarde
Born: 1567
Marr: 1590
Died: 17 Feb 1633

Sir Walter DEVEREUX
Born: aft 1566
Died: 1591

Margaret DAKYNS
Lady Devereux, Lady Hoby
Born: bef 10 Feb 1571
Marr: 1587 (app.)
Died: 4 Sep 1633

TUDOR TIMES
© Tudor Times Ltd 2015

Lady Penelope Devereux' Life Story

Chapter 1: Childhood & Youth (1563 – 1581)

Lady Penelope Devereux was born into a family high in the favour of Elizabeth I. Her mother's family were blood relatives of the Queen: her grandmother, Katherine Carey, being the daughter of Mary Boleyn, Elizabeth's aunt. Katherine was a great favourite with the Queen all her life, and her husband, Sir Francis Knollys, was one of Elizabeth's chief ministers until his death in 1596. The Knollys' daughter, Lettice, had been a maid-of-honour to the Queen until marrying Penelope's father, Walter Devereux, Viscount Hereford in around 1561.

Penelope's paternal family, the Devereux, although not so closely related to the Queen as the Knollys, were, like most members of the aristocracy descended from Edward III and Penelope's grandfather and great-grandfather had received favour from Henry VIII. Both the Knollys and the Devereux families had embraced the Reformation with vigour.

Penelope spent her early childhood at Chartley Manor in Staffordshire, eldest of a family of four (a fifth child died young). Her surviving siblings were Robert, Walter and Dorothy. In the fashion of the time, Penelope and Dorothy received a thorough education, of a level that in earlier, and later, times, would have been confined to the sons of the family. Penelope's tutor was Mathias Homes, a Cambridge man of strong Protestant views. She studied French, Spanish and Italian, as well as the courtly accomplishments of dancing, singing and playing the lute.

Penelope's father was zealous in the service of the Queen, being one of Mary, Queen of Scots' custodians, and instrumental in the suppression of the Rebellion of the Northern Earls in 1569. In recognition of his merits, he was granted the Earldom of Essex in 1572. The following year, Elizabeth gave Essex a licence to colonise Ulster in Ireland, controlled by the O'Neills and the Scots. The venture was undertaken at his own cost, and was a disaster, militarily, financially and personally. He returned to England in 1575, with a view to rebuilding his fortunes at home, but in September of that year was created Earl Marshal of Ireland a post necessitating a return to Ireland. He arrived in Dublin in September 1576, but died within a few weeks, of dysentery.

Her father's will left dowries of £2,000 each for Penelope and Dorothy, but the disastrous Irish expedition had left his estates impoverished, and payment of these dowries would be a serious burden on the inheritance of his son, Robert, now the 2nd Earl. In regard to Penelope's marriage, the Earl had expressed a wish for her to marry Philip Sidney, the nephew of Robert Dudley, Earl of Leicester, Queen Elizabeth's favourite. Philip had been with Essex in Ireland and Essex had conceived a great affection for the younger man. There was no formal agreement prior to Essex' death, and Sidney's father, Sir Henry Sidney was not in favour of the match. Sir Henry, who was Lord Deputy of Ireland, had disagreed with Essex' policies there, and disliked him personally. This, coupled with the fact that Penelope was not yet of marriageable age, meant the match went into abeyance.

With their father dead, the wardship of the Devereux children was now at the Queen's disposal. Essex had expressed a wish for his heir, Robert, to be placed in the guardianship of Sir William Cecil, Lord Burghley, whilst Penelope was to be put in the care of Essex' cousin, Henry Hastings, 3rd Earl of Huntingdon and his wife, Katherine Dudley. Such arrangements were perfectly usual, and in no way expressed a distrust of his wife, Lettice.

Although Huntingdon had a respectable claim to the throne as the great-grandson of Margaret Plantagenet, Countess of Salisbury, and the grandson of Henry Pole, Baron Montague, who had been executed in the Exeter Conspiracy, Elizabeth I trusted him, and he was her Lord Lieutenant of the North. Penelope's home was now the King's Manor at York.

Lady Huntingdon was not only the sister of the powerful Robert Dudley, Earl of Leicester, but also the aunt of Penelope's intended bridegroom, Philip Sidney. Although she had no children of her own, Lady Huntingdon was renowned for her management and upbringing of young gentlewomen. Both the Earl and Countess were committed Puritans, and the household lived under a rather stringent regime of daily prayers, Bible readings and sermons, which Penelope's later career suggests she may have found rather onerous.

Not long after Penelope left for York, her mother, Lettice, married the Earl of Leicester. When Queen Elizabeth discovered the marriage, she was furious, and Lettice was banned from court for the rest of her life. Nevertheless, Elizabeth was not inclined to blame Lettice's children for her misdemeanours, and Lady Huntingdon brought Penelope to court, presenting her at Whitehall on 30th January 1581.

Chapter 2: Court & Marriage (1581 – 1590)

During 1581, Penelope was in close attendance on the Queen. It was a period of extravagant display, as Elizabeth, for the last time, entertained thoughts of marriage, on this occasion with the French Prince, the Duc d'Alencon. There were masques and jousts to attend, and even the celebrations surrounding the return of Francis Drake from his circumnavigation of the globe. The whole court attended at Deptford when Elizabeth knighted him. However, as Penelope was now eighteen, and was not formally appointed to the role of maid-of-honour to the Queen, the time had come for her marriage to be arranged.

Philip Sidney was struck off the list by her guardian. From having been the heir to both his uncles (the Earls of Warwick and Leicester), he had now been supplanted by Penelope's new half-brother, Robert Dudley, Lord Denbigh. Sidney was therefore not a particularly good prospect for the daughter of an Earl, and Penelope's dowry was somewhat in doubt.

Instead, Huntingdon proposed a marriage with Robert, 3rd Baron Rich, a major landholder in Essex, and of a similar age to Penelope. Rich, as a second son, had inherited unexpectedly. Not anticipating that he would become a Baron, he had entered the House of Commons representing Essex on 2nd February, 1581, then inherited the Barony (which debarred him from the Commons) on 27th February the same year. Lord Rich would have appealed to Huntingdon as he was a radical Puritan, supporting Calvinist preachers, and later, running into disputes with the conservative John Aylmer, Bishop of London.

Penelope and Lord Rich were married in the autumn of 1581. There was trouble over her dowry, as the Essex estates were still in dire financial straits. Her grandfather, Sir Francis Knollys, assisted to the tune of £500. It was later claimed that Penelope had protested against her marriage, and that Rich was a harsh husband, but, since the source was her second husband, it may be prejudiced. It is certainly the case that Lord Rich was less well-educated than his wife, so perhaps they did not have a great deal in common. Nevertheless, personal compatibility, although desirable, was not the primary motive for a marriage and it seems unlikely that Penelope would have expected to marry for love.

Whatever Penelope's thoughts as a young bride, she was able to continue her life at court in the immediate aftermath of her wedding.

She appears to have taken the court by storm. Her looks, charm and grace were praised both then, and for the rest of her life. She seems to have had a beauty and charisma that did not fade with age or repeated childbearing. Her most famous conquest was none other than the Philip Sidney her father had intended her to marry. She was the inspiration for his sonnet cycle *'Astrophil and Stella'*. Whether the relationship ever became more than one of courtly sighing and hand-kissing cannot be known for certain, but there is no evidence for anything more.

Penelope spent the next few years between the Rich's London home at St Bartholomew's and their estates in Essex, primarily at Leez Priory. She maintained a copious correspondence with her mother and her siblings, being particularly close to her brother, Robert, 2nd Earl of Essex, naming her second daughter after him – Essex Rich.

Chapter 3: War & Intrigue (1585 – 1595)

Penelope's brother, the young Earl of Essex was growing in favour with the Queen, promoted by his step-father, Leicester. In 1585, Elizabeth, after years of importuning by the Puritan party at court, finally agreed to aid the Protestant Netherlands against the Catholic Philip of Spain, who was the hereditary ruler. Leicester led an army onto Flanders, and Essex and Philip Sidney accompanied him. Initially, Leicester had asked for Penelope's husband, Lord Rich, to take part, *'though he be no man of war'* but in the event, Leicester changed his plans and Rich remained at home.

Sidney died at Zutphen, and became the stuff of legend. Essex, to whom he bequeathed his sword, married his widow, and attempted to emulate Sidney's glory. We cannot know whether Penelope felt anything stronger on the death of Sidney than the general outpouring of grief that accompanied his passing. The tale that, on his death bed, he confessed to adultery with her, has been shown to have no contemporary basis.

Following his return from the Netherlands, Essex rose rapidly in Elizabeth's favour, taking on Leicester's role as Master of the Horse, and spending long hours with the queen, gambling, playing cards, dancing, and, ominously, quarrelling vociferously with her.

The war in the Netherlands rumbled on, and Spain sought revenge for Elizabeth's interference. Rumours grew of a huge armada to be sent against England. Lord Rich was responsible for the militia in Essex, whilst Leicester and Essex were with the Queen at Tilbury. Penelope was probably either at Leez or with her mother at the Leicesters' home at Wanstead.

The strain of the Armada campaign was too much for Leicester, and to the great grief of his wife, and Penelope, as well as the Queen, he died shortly after. Lord Rich attended the funeral, as did Sir Christopher Blount who had been Master of the Horse to Leicester, and within the year was to comfort the grieving widow. He and Lettice were married in early 1589, giving Penelope a second step-father, who was also a close friend of her brother.

In October 1589, Penelope, Lord Rich and Essex entered into a correspondence that was at best foolish, and at worst, treason. They wrote to King James VI of Scotland, pledging their support for his succession to the English crown, which, they hinted, could not be long in coming. Penelope, who had the code name 'Rialta', even sent him a miniature of herself. King James seems to have been rather circumspect in his responses. He knew he was Elizabeth's preferred successor, and was too wily a hand to risk annoying her (and losing the pension she paid him) by trying to step into her shoes before time.

Penelope's reasons for embroiling herself in such a risky undertaking can only be guessed at. Her biographer, Sally Varlow, suggests her actions were justified, as Elizabeth's failure to promote Essex to a prime place in government, together with Elizabeth's continued harshness towards Lettice, were symptoms of a corrupt government that did not deserve their long-term loyalty. A less partisan view might be that Penelope and Essex, for all their intellectual brilliance were politically naïve, and were demonstrating the factionalism that was to dog the last decade and a half of Elizabeth's reign. Although Elizabeth was deeply attached to Essex, she did not rate his political skills particularly highly, and, taking the long view of her reign, she seems to have been an excellent judge of character.

At some time during the early 1590s Penelope began an affair with Sir Charles Blount, a friend of Essex (and distant relative of her step-father). Blount was a military man who had seen action in the Netherlands and in the Armada engagement. On his first coming to Court, Essex had seen him as a rival for royal favour, and had insulted him, provoking a duel. Blount won a swift victory, wounding his opponent in the thigh, and the two became fast friends. In the early days of Blount's affair with Penelope, they kept the relationship quiet, but she bore him at least three children, possibly five, all of whom were accepted by Lord Rich as his own, although he cannot have been in much doubt about their paternity. Penelope even named her son Mountjoy, the title Blount inherited in 1594. Given that Rich was protecting her from public shame by accepting her children, this seems a rather tasteless choice.

Chapter 4: The Jesuit Mission (1594)

Any biography of Robert Devereux, Earl of Essex characterises him as rash, impetuous, a risk-taker and of poor judgement. It would seem that

Penelope had some of the same characteristics. Not content with a potentially treasonable correspondence with the King of Scots, and an affair that was obvious to anyone who knew her, Penelope was also involved in the far more serious business of harbouring a Catholic priest.

By the 1590s, it was treason for any Englishman to be ordained as a priest in the Roman Catholic Church or for any Jesuit or priest ordained after the Queen's accession, to be in England. It was a crime to hear the Catholic mass, and it was a crime to harbour or give succour to any priest.

The Government was at pains to explain that persecution was not for the matter of being Catholic, but for the political dimensions of support for Spanish invasion and undermining of the Queen's legitimate rule. Persons caught harbouring a priest would be subject to fines, confiscations, imprisonment, and potentially, for repeated offences, death.

Despite this, Penelope hid Father John Gerard, one of the most important men in the Catholic hierarchy in England, in her own house at Leez. Gerard had been staying with the Wiseman family at Braddocks Manor, near Thaxted. The Wisemans were connections of Lord Rich, and despite their very different religious beliefs, Penelope was godmother to one of the Wiseman children. Mrs Wiseman, after one of the raids on her house, spent time with Penelope at Leez, and arranged for her to receive Gerard. He came to Leez in the early spring of 1594, in the guise of a visiting friend.

According to his later account, Penelope was close to conversion, but wanted to consult Mountjoy. Mountjoy, a man of intellect and education, prepared questions for Father Gerard, with the assurance that if they could be answered satisfactorily, he, too, would convert. Whether the answers were unconvincing, or the risk was too high, Mountjoy, and hence Penelope, remained unreconciled to Rome but she seems to have remained sympathetic to the Catholic cause, a position which, later, endeared her to Queen Anne of Denmark.

At this distance, we cannot know whether Penelope's interest was religiously motivated, whether she was a natural risk-taker and wanted to provoke her husband and family, who were largely on the Puritan end of Protestantism, or whether she was taking up a chic cause. It certainly appears that the young and fashionable court circles of the 1590s flirted with Catholicism, perhaps as a natural reaction to the control that Burghley, Walsingham, Knollys and the rest of the staunchly Protestant old guard exerted. It may be that she was naturally compassionate and sought to save Gerard from the dreadful death he would have suffered had he been caught by the authorities. (He was later caught, imprisoned, tortured, and escaped.)

Chapter 5: Penelope & Essex (1590 – 1600)

Penelope's relationship with her brother was always close. During the 1590s, as she spent less time at Leez, and pursued her relationship with Mountjoy, she took on a role as Essex' chief supporter, friend and hostess. Her sister-in-law, Frances Walsingham, who had previously been married to Sir Philip Sidney, seems to have happily taken a more retired position. Frances was regularly pregnant, but suffered several miscarriages and infant deaths, as well as having to tolerate a husband who was a notorious philanderer.

In 1593, Essex became one of Elizabeth's Privy Councillors, yet he was not satisfied. He wished to supplant the Cecils in Elizabeth's favour, and, aided by Penelope, spent much time and money building up an information network (or spy-ring, depending on your point of view) across England, France and Spain. He too, despite the strongly

Protestant background from which he and Penelope came, was flirting with the many disaffected Catholics who had been given new courage by the Jesuit mission.

During the 1590s both Essex and Mountjoy were involved in military campaigns. Finally, in 1599, Essex took command of the campaign in Ireland, which proved as disastrous for him as it had for his father. He disobeyed direct commands from the Queen, and wasted money and men. He returned to England, in contravention of orders, and was questioned by the Privy Council in a five-hour session, that concluded that he had deserted his post, and made a dishonourable truce with O'Neill leader of the Irish rebels (as the English government characterised them).

Essex was committed to house arrest at one of his London homes, York House. Whilst he was confined there, he suffered some illness, perhaps a fever caught on campaign, or perhaps stress-induced. Both Penelope and her sister, Dorothy, now Countess of Northumberland (after a secret first marriage that had brought down the wrath of the Queen), received permission to wait upon the Queen to beg permission for him to move to somewhere with 'better air' and to be allowed to see him. Making a show of mourning by dressing in black from head to foot, they went to Richmond. The Queen received them kindly, but she would not budge. Penelope continued to plead, sending letters, presents and jewels to the Queen, which the Queen accepted, without changing her mind.

Eventually, one of Penelope's letters went too far. Her enthusiasm for her brother's cause, and her conviction that the Cecils were up to no good, was read as a hint that rebellion was in the air, and she was summoned before the Lord Treasurer, Sir Thomas Sackville, later Earl of Dorset, to explain her actions. She hastily followed up with another letter to the Queen, protesting loyalty. Not long after, she was accused of having allowed copies of the earlier, suspect, letter, to be distributed and was summoned again to the Privy Council. Taken ill, either really, or politically, she was excused attendance, and retired to the country. Her distress was probably added to by the dispatch of Mountjoy to Ireland to replace Essex. Penelope was again interrogated about her offending letter, but the Queen, at length, forgave her, whilst complaining that she 'showed a proud disposition' and had been very negligent in allowing her correspondence to be circulated.

At last, it appeared that the Queen would forgive Essex too and he was released from house arrest in August 1600. But this was not a complete restoration - Elizabeth refused to renew his main source of income, the monopoly on sweet wines, which had been granted in 1589.

Financially ruined, and increasingly paranoid, Essex fortified Essex House, with his wife, Frances, and Penelope in support. After taking several Privy Councillors hostage, Essex, together with his chief supporters, the Earl of Southampton and Penelope's step-father, Sir Christopher Blount, rode through the streets of London, trying to gain followers to overthrow the Cecils, whom he continued to blame for his disfavour with the Queen. The Londoners were underwhelmed and Essex retreated to his house, sending Penelope and Frances away.

Essex was captured and sent to the Tower and Penelope was placed under house arrest with Sir Henry Sackford. Following his trial (in which Lord Rich was one of the judges), Essex was adjudged guilty. Afterwards, he requested that members of the Council be sent to the Tower to hear the 'truth'. This consisted of denouncing both Mountjoy and Penelope whom, he claimed, had pushed him into treason:

'I must accuse one who is most nearest to me, my sister who did continually urge me on...'

He added that 'she must be looked to, for she hath a proud spirit.'

This disloyalty must have been an agonising blow to Penelope who herself remained under house arrest, and was questioned by the Privy Council. During her interrogation she pointed out that, far from being the instigator of Essex' treason, she had:

'been more like a slave than a sister, which proceeded out of my exceeding love, rather than his authority'

Essex was executed on 25th February 1601, together with Sir Christopher Blount, Penelope's step-father. Eventually released, Penelope herself was sent home to her husband. Meanwhile, Mountjoy had been running the most successful campaign in Ireland of the whole Tudor era, whilst secretly corresponding with King James.

Chapter 6: Court Favourite (1603 – 1605)

The covert correspondence with James VI of Scotland at last paid off. When Elizabeth finally died on 24th March 1603, Penelope was chosen by the new king to travel to Berwick to accompany his wife, Anne of Denmark, south to her new kingdom. Penelope was some eleven years older than the new Queen, but they formed a very warm relationship and she was appointed as one of the Queen's most senior attendants. In a sign that the Devereux were now back in favour, James permitted the late Earl's three children to be restored in blood, and receive their father's estates.

Penelope was so high in favour with both King and Queen, that, on 17th August 1603, at a ceremony at Farnham Castle, she was given the rank of the Earldom of Essex, in the seniority it had had under the Bourchier earls. This elevation gave her rank above all the baronesses, and most of the Earls' daughters. Penelope's great-great grandmother, Cecily Bourchier, had been the grand-daughter of the 1st Earl of Essex.

Over the next three years, Penelope became one of the leading lights in the Jacobean court, taking part in the elaborate masques and entertainments that Queen Anne patronised.

Mountjoy, having brought the Irish war to a successful conclusion (from the English perspective), returned to London in 1603, and received the title of Earl of Devonshire from James I as well as being appointed as a Privy Councillor. He and Penelope now lived together openly.

In 1605, Lord Rich sought a divorce from the Church Commissioners. Whether he chose to instigate proceedings because the open cohabitation of Penelope and Mountjoy was a step too far, or whether Penelope requested the divorce, which is the contention of her biographer, Sally Varlow, is unknown.

The divorce was granted on 14th November 1605, on the grounds of Lady Rich's adultery with a man whom she refused to name in court. Archbishop Bancroft, pronouncing the sentence even went so far as to condemn Lord Rich for his hardness to his wife, and made derogatory remarks about Rich's Puritan leanings.

As the marriage had been legal, and produced off-spring, the divorce was *from bed and board*, rather than an annulment, which would have required an Act of Parliament. The Church of England, whilst permitting divorce, did not allow remarriage during the life-time of the other partner (a position that remained unchanged until 2002) and both Penelope and Lord Rich were ordered to live celibate lives.

Penelope and Devonshire immediately flouted the Church's rules and went through a marriage ceremony conducted by Devonshire's chaplain, William Laud, (later Archbishop of Canterbury) on 26th December 1605. This action called down a storm of anger and retribution on their heads.

King James, angered that they had defied the law, banished Penelope from court, telling Devonshire he had won '*a fair woman with a black soul.*' Devonshire now wrote to James, explaining why he believed the marriage to be legal. One of his arguments was that Penelope had not freely consented to her marriage to Rich. Free consent was a fundamental requirement for valid matrimony. James remained unconvinced and Penelope remained banished.

In the Spring of 1606, Devonshire, as a Privy Councillor, was obliged to attend the trials of the Gunpowder Plotters, many of whom were members of Penelope's extended family. In particular, her sister's husband, the Earl of Northumberland, was a prime suspect, despite all of the other plotters denying he was involved. At the end of March, Devonshire failed to make an appearance at the trial of the Jesuit, Father Garnet. His health was had been ruined by his campaigning, and he had been taken ill at Wanstead.

Penelope, pregnant again, raced to join him, and he spent his last days trying to protect the inheritance of their children. He died on 3rd April 1607, aged forty-three, with Penelope at his side. The shock and grief caused Penelope to miscarry.

Devonshire's record of service in Ireland was not forgotten, and he was given a ceremonious funeral at Westminster Abbey, followed to his grave by the Earl of Southampton (who had narrowly escaped execution with Essex), Suffolk and Nottingham. In a clear sign that his marriage to Penelope was not recognised, her arms were not shown quartered with his, as was customary for a wife.

Prior to their marriage, Devonshire had created complex legal and financial arrangements that would enable his children by Penelope to inherit his estates. The desire for a legal heir, which was so central to sixteenth century thought, may well have been a motivating factor in their speedy marriage.

As Devonshire had anticipated, his Will and property settlements were hotly contested. Various members of the Blount family, who saw an opportunity for taking control of Devonshire's vast estate, suggested that he had been unduly influenced; that he was not of sound mind; and that he regretted his relationship with Penelope.

Probate was granted in the Canterbury Court, then appealed, then confirmed again. Eventually, a charge of fraud was brought against Penelope in the Star Chamber (the Privy Council and senior judges in session). She was described as '*an harlot, adulteress, concubine and whore*'.

Before the matter was settled, Penelope died on 6th July 1607. The location is unknown, but it was probably Essex House. Conflicting stories circulated – one that she had regretted her liaison with Devonshire, and wished to be reconciled to Lord Rich, dying firmly in the Protestant religion she had been brought up in. Father Gerard, however, claimed that, at the last, she converted to the Catholic faith.

*

Penelope was later described by Archbishop Laud as '*A lady in whom lodged all attractive graces of beauty, wit and sweetness of behaviour*' and it is very apparent that she was able to charm both men and women, being beloved by her family, friends and servants. Nevertheless, it is hard to escape from the conclusion that she was also rash and spoilt, unable to perceive that there might be other priorities than the advancement of her family, or the indulgence of her desires.

Aspects of Lady Penelope Devereux' Life

Chapter 7: Poetry & Patronage

Elizabeth I's court was the centre of a great flowering of literature, music and drama with the Queen herself being an accomplished musician and a fair hand at writing verse. The courtiers with whom she surrounded herself were expected to be able to provide intellectual amusement and stimulation, not just administrative or military prowess. This emphasis on culture led to the patronage by leading courtiers of painters, poets, playwrights and actors.

This patronage was similar to that already extended by higher members of society to their lower-ranking '*clients*' and might take the form of money, advancement to posts in the patron's gift, help in legal matters, or support for advantageous marriages. In return, the artist (usually, but not always, men) would dedicate his work to the patron. The higher ranking your patron was, the better chance you had of selling your work and being recognised, so artists were always seeking recognition from the elite.

When Penelope Devereux came to court in the 1580s, other courtiers who were at the centre of the cultural life of the court included Mary Sidney, Countess of Pembroke, and her brother, Sir Philip Sidney, whom Penelope's father, the Earl of Essex had wished her to marry. Essex described Sidney as

'so wise, so virtuous, so goodly; and if he go on in the course that he hath begun, he will be as famous and worthy a gentleman as ever England bred' and expressed the hope that 'if God do move both their hearts ... he might match with my daughter [Penelope].'

The Sidney siblings (who were also niece and nephew to Penelope's step-father, the Earl of Leicester) were two of the most talented members of the court. The Countess gave patronage to the poets Michael Drayton, Ben Jonson, Edmund Spenser and many others, as well as writing and translating herself, and completing works unfinished at Philip's death.

Both Philip Sidney and the Countess were dedicatees of literary works, he receiving some forty dedications, and she a few less. In fact, the Countess of Pembroke received the second highest number of dedications to a non-royal woman of the whole Elizabethan and Jacobean era, preceded only by Lucy Russell (nee Harington), Countess of Bedford.

By 1581. when Penelope appeared at court, Philip, then aged 27, had already produced '*The Lady of May*' dedicated to the Queen, and the first version of *Arcadia* – a 180,000 word romance he referred to as a '*trifle*' – and he was now about to embark on a sonnet cycle which took Penelope Devereux as its heroine.

Whether he was actually in love with her, or whether she seemed a suitable subject – she was fair-haired, dark eyed, and beautiful – is unsure. It seems unlikely that he would compose sonnets featuring someone to whom he was completely indifferent, but, of course, admiring a court beauty who was married to another man is not the same as being in love.

The cycle of sonnets, 108 in number, was entitled '*Astrophil and Stella*'. The poet tells of his attraction to the lady, who is, of course, unattainable, and his struggles to overcome it, before dedicating himself to public service. The work was not initially printed, but circulated in manuscript form until published in 1591, after Sidney's death.

Penelope has been recognised as the heroine from the frequent use of the word '*rich*', her married name, and juxtapositions of the word implying her husband, Lord Rich (who was, as it happened, extremely wealthy) did not deserve her:

But that rich fool who by blind Fortune's lot
The richest gem of love and life enjoys,
And can with foul abuse such beauties blot;
Let him, depriv'd of sweet but unfelt joys,
(Exil'd for aye from those high treasures, which
He knows not) grow in only folly rich.

From Sonnet 24 – Astrophil and Stella – Sir Philip Sidney

There is no record of Penelope's reaction to the sonnets – but it is hard to imagine that any woman of nineteen would be less than charmed and flattered by being the focus of a man who was much admired at court. Her feelings for Sidney are unknown – the convention of the sonnet cycle is that she should disdain his love. There is certainly no evidence that she had any illicit relationship with him.

As well as being Sidney's muse, Penelope inspired or was the dedicatee of other works. It is argued in '*Sir Philip Sidney and the Circulation of Manuscripts, 1558-1640*' by H R Woudhysen that she was the inspiration for several of the secular songs written by the famous Elizabethan composer, William Byrd. More certainly, Edward Paston dedicated his translation of '*Diana*' by the Spanish writer, Montemayor, to her and the lutenist Charles Tessier set several of the Astrophil sonnets to music.

Penelope's interest and involvement in culture continued, and she was closely associated with the extravagant patronage extended by Queen Anne of Denmark in the early 1600s.

Chapter 8: Queen Anne's Masques

Anne of Denmark became Queen of Scots in 1589; and Queen of England when her husband succeeded Elizabeth in March 1603. As Anne was pregnant at the time of James' accession to the English throne, she did not immediately accompany him south, instead, remaining in Scotland with a view to travelling when she was delivered. Sadly, the pregnancy ended in a miscarriage in May 1603. Soon after, she set out for her new kingdom.

James had arranged for a number of great ladies of the English court to meet the Queen, one of whom was Penelope Devereux, Lady Rich, who had been in secret contact with James since the 1580s.

Anne appears to have taken an immediate liking to Lady Rich, although she was some eleven years older than the 29 year old Queen. Anne also became intimate with the younger Lucy, Countess of Bedford, whom she selected as her chief Lady of the Bedchamber. Lady Bedford and Penelope were well acquainted, as Lucy and her husband had been intimates of Essex, and Lord Bedford had been involved in the rebellion of 1600.

Penelope, too was appointed to the Queen's service.

Queen Anne, like Penelope and Lady Bedford, was an avid patron of poetry and theatrical works. The Queen commissioned works, and all three ladies were dedicatees of poetry and prose. In particular, Anne was a patron of the masque – a stylised hybrid of play, ballet, musical interlude and poetry.

The playwright, Ben Jonson, wrote his first work for the Queen in June 1603, when he penned a welcome for her and Prince Henry, to be recited at the arrival at Sir Robert Spencer's home at Althorp,

Northamptonshire (Sir Robert was an ancestor of the late Diana, Princess of Wales).

Thereafter, with the exception of 1604, Jonson wrote all of the Christmas masques for the court, and worked closely with the architect, Inigo Jones, as set designer.

The budget for clothes, for dancing masters, for instruments and musicians was enormous. The first two masques – 'The Twelve Goddesses' of 1604 and the 'Masque of Blackness' of 1605 cost some £2,000 each. The scenery was complex and elaborate.

Whilst the singing and recitation were generally performed by professional actors, the dancing was undertaken by members of the Court, from the Queen downward. To be asked to take part was a great honour, as the standard of dancing and acting was high – these were not family Christmas games, with everyone laughing if a player tripped or stood on his partner's toe. The masques were intended to demonstrate the wealth and power of the two crowns of England and Scotland. Observers from foreign courts were impressed by the extravagance of the spectacles the Queen arranged

'in everyone's opinion no other Court could have displayed such pomp and riches' reported the Venetian Ambassador about the Christmas masque of 1604.

The evening usually opened with the 'antemasque' which was intended to look like an amateur romp, with bawdy dancing and low humour – perhaps rather in the style of the play in 'A Midsummer Night's Dream'. Then the masque proper would begin, with formal dancing, created from intricate choreography which had been practised for weeks, accompanied by viols or lutes. Finally, the masque participants would dance familiar court dances, such as the galliard, with members of the audience.

Penelope Devereux took part in at least two masques, the first being *'The Vision of the Twelve Goddesses'*, by Samuel Daniel produced for Christmas 1603. It was performed on Sunday, 8th January, 1604, at Hampton Court.

The masque opened with Night requesting her son Somnus to send a dream to the courtiers. They were to see a Temple of Peace with the priestess, Sybil. Iris, the god's messenger, then appeared to Sybil, telling her that twelve goddesses were about to appear. The ladies came in threes, preceded by the Three Graces. The first wave of goddesses was Queen Anne as Pallas, the Countess of Suffolk as Juno, and Penelope as Venus.

The goddesses danced *'with majestie and arte'*, forming squares, triangles and circles. They then selected gentlemen from the audience to dance with, before retiring back to the heavens.

The second masque in which Penelope took part was the *'Masque of Blackness'*, commissioned by Queen Anne for Twelfth Night 1605. Her instruction to Ben Jonson, was that she wished her ladies and herself to be disguised as 'blackamoors'. Their costumes were of blue, silver and pearl, and they were made up with black face-paint.

The scene opens with the Queen and her ladies sitting in a sea-shell, representing the water goddesses who are the daughters of the god Niger, and grand-daughters of Oceanus. Oceanus and Niger discuss the fact that the goddesses, who are supremely beautiful, have been upset to learn that the northern poets prefer fair-skinned beauties.

Niger has tried to reassure them, pointing out (with a level of cultural sensitivity that perhaps may surprise us) that they are perfect as they are, and should not seek to bind themselves to European ideas of beauty. Nevertheless, the water-goddesses resolve to ask the moon-goddess Aethiopia for help. She recommends moving to less sunny climes, suggesting places ending in –atania. The water goddesses have tried moving to Acquitania, Lusitania and Mauretania, but to no avail. *(I think we can see where this is going...Ed.)*

At this point the water-goddesses dance in pairs.

Niger begs Aethiopia to help again, as his daughters have been such faithful worshippers. She appears and tells them to visit Britannia, where the wisdom of the sun-lit King represents such a light of Reason, that it will whiten even a black-skinned Aethiopian. The water-goddesses are to travel to Britannia, and the light of his countenance will transform them. More practically, they are to bathe once a month in sea-dew, and in a year, when they return, they will be white.

The water-goddesses then dance with the audience.

Penelope's role was Ocyte, the water-goddess representing swiftness, and her partner was Katherine Knyvett, the Countess of Suffolk, whose first husband had been Lord Rich's elder brother.

Penelope's inclusion in these extravagant events is a testament to her grace, skill in dance, and beauty, as well as to her warm relationship with the Queen.

Chapter 9: Following the Footsteps of Penelope Devereux

In common with the vast majority of women of the Tudor period, Lady Penelope Devereux never travelled abroad. She did, however, travel frequently and reasonably extensively within England and Wales.

The numbers in the article below correspond to those on the map which follows.

Penelope was born at Chartley Manor (1) in Staffordshire, a modern house built after the Battle of Bosworth. It was constructed in the grounds of the twelfth century Chartley Castle, which was considered old fashioned and uncomfortable. During the 1580s, when Chartley was owned by Penelope's brother, Mary, Queen of Scots was imprisoned there, but it is very unlikely that Penelope would ever have seen her. Today, the original manor house has disappeared, and what was formally the home farm is now called Chartley Manor Farm. Ruins of the castle remain.

Penelope's father, the Earl of Essex, was an extensive landowner in South Wales and the Marches, and it is probable that Penelope visited the Bishop's Palace at Llandyfai (Lamfey) in Pembrokeshire (2) where her father spent a good deal of his time, as did her brother, Robert, 2nd Earl of Essex, in the 1580s. Today, the Bishop's Palace is an impressive ruin, in the care of Cadw, the Welsh heritage body.

During her childhood, and later, Penelope would also have spent a good deal of time at Blithfield Hall (pronounced Blifield), Staffordshire (3), the home of the Bagot family, who acted as agents, factors and personal attendants to the Devereux. The Hall of the Penelope's day has been somewhat embellished, but remains in the hands of the Bagot family. It is not open to the public.

In the aftermath of her father's death, Penelope's mother, Lettice Knollys, took Penelope and her sister, Dorothy, to the houses of various different friends and relatives. One of the main locations where Penelope spent time then, and later, was Grey's Court, near Rotherfield Greys in Oxfordshire (8). Originally owned by the Grey family, it was granted to Robert Knollys in 1514, and completely remodelled by Penelope's grandfather, Sir Francis Knollys. He and his wife, Elizabeth I's cousin Katherine Carey, lived there when they were not at court. It is now in the hands of the National Trust.

Around a year after her father's death, Penelope became the ward of the Earl of Huntingdon, and travelled north to his home at King's Manor,

York (4). Formerly the Abbot's House at the Abbey of St Mary, York, the property had been turned into a private residence at the dissolution of the Monasteries, some forty years previously. Today King's Manor is a conference centre.

In 1578, Penelope's mother married again. Her husband, Robert Dudley, Earl of Leicester, was Queen Elizabeth's most favoured friend and courtier, and possessed of extensive land and property. Penelope was close to her mother and step-father and, through the course of their marriage, spent considerable amounts of time at Leicester's various properties.

The principle property that denoted Leicester's wealth and status was the magnificent Kenilworth Castle (5), a few miles north of Warwick. It is unlikely that Penelope was at the extravagant entertainment that Leicester staged for Elizabeth at Kenilworth in 1575, but she would no doubt have heard about it.

The other properties Leicester owned were Wanstead House (6), that he had bought from Lord Rich, whom Penelope was to marry, and Leicester House (7), in the Strand. Both of these properties were to figure large in Penelope's life. She frequently visited Wanstead when it was her mother's home, and later, it is where she spent most of her short married life with the man she considered to be her second husband. After Leicester's death, Leicester House became the property of Penelope's brother, Robert Devereux, Earl of Essex, and, with great originality, was renamed Essex House. Penelope was at Essex House with her brother when he mounted his foolish attempted coup against the Cecils, which ended in disaster and execution. None of these houses remain.

When Penelope married for the first time in 1581, her principle homes were Leez (or Leighs) Priory, Essex (9) – now a rather sumptuous country house hotel - and a town house near St Bartholomew's in London (12). This had been part of the Priory of that name, but had been granted to Penelope's father-in-law, the notorious Sir Richard Rich whose perjury had condemned Sir Thomas More. No trace remains of this property. Lord and Lady Rich, as Penelope was now styled, also owned Rochford Hall, Essex (11), which was the main residence of her widowed mother-in-law, and coincidentally, had probably been the married home of her own great-grandmother, Mary Boleyn. Rochford Hall still stands, partially a golf club, with some residential properties.

Penelope also frequently visited the Walsingham home in Seething Lane, London (13). Sir Francis Walsingham's daughter, Frances, married Penelope's brother, the Earl of Essex, and the two women seem to have been friends, with Penelope visiting frequently, and acting as godmother to Frances' children.

After Leicester's death, Lettice married for a third time, but was again widowed when her husband, Sir Christopher Blount, lost his head alongside her son, the Earl of Essex. Following this double tragedy, she spent a good deal of time at Drayton Bassett (11) in Staffordshire, not far from Chartley, and Penelope visited her there regularly. Penelope however, although singing small after Essex' death for the rest of Elizabeth's reign, came into her full glory in 1603 with the accession of James VI of Scotland to the English throne.

Throughout the 1580s and 1590s the Devereux siblings had been maintaining covert links with James, and the effort now paid off. Penelope was sent to Berwick-upon-Tweed (14) to greet the new Queen, Anne of Denmark, as she crossed into her new kingdom. The Queen was charmed with Penelope, who became one of her ladies of the Bedchamber, and returned to a full court life, living at Whitehall, Richmond, Hampton Court and the other royal palaces.

In 1603, at Farnham Castle (15), Penelope was raised to the rank of the earldom of Essex, despite being only the wife of a Baron. In the status conscious 1600s this was a significant mark of royal favour. In this case, however, pride came before a resounding fall. Penelope's illegal second marriage to her long-time lover, the Earl of Devonshire, horrified the King, and she was banished from Court.

She spent most of the short period of life left to her at Wanstead House, before dying in July 1607. Her places of death and burial are unknown, although both probably occurred within the environs of London.

Key to Map

1. Chartley Manor, Staffordshire
2. Bishop's Palace, Lamphey (Llandyfai), Pembroke
3. Blithfield, Staffordshire
4. King's Manor, York
5. Kenilworth Castle, Warwickshire
6. Wanstead House, Essex
7. Leicester (later Essex) House, The Strand, London
8. Greys Court, Rotherfield Greys, Oxfordshire
9. Leighs (Leez) Priory, Essex
10. Drayton Manor, Drayton Bassett, Staffordshire
11. Rochford Hall, Essex
12. St Bartholomew house, nr St Bartholomew-the-Great Church, London
13. Walsingham House, Seething Lane, London
14. Berwick-upon-Tweed
15. Farnham Castle, Surrey

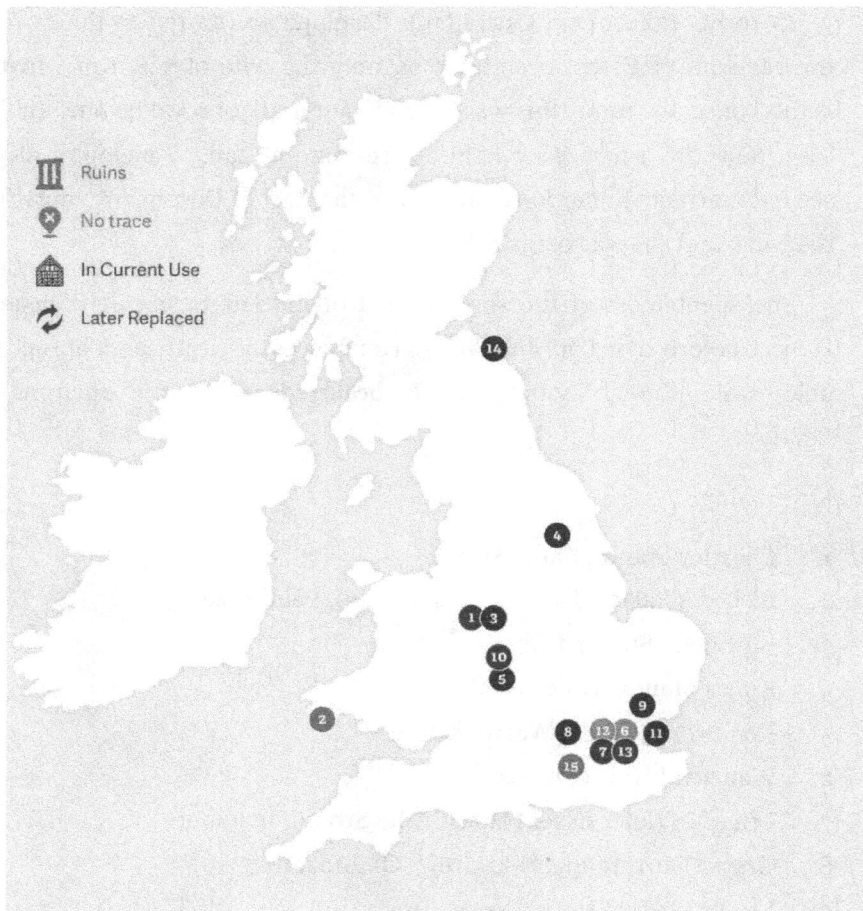

Chapter 10: Book Review

Surprisingly, there are few biographies of Penelope – seen as a disgrace to her sex, she has been overlooked by writers for four hundred years. Sally Varlow's extremely detailed biography is the first modern work.

The Lady Penelope

Author: Sally Varlow

Publisher: Deutsch

In a nutshell: A wealth of facts, and very readable, but marred by its partisan perspective and fictional style.

There was a lot to like in this book. Prior to reading it, I knew very little about Lady Penelope Devereux, other than that she was the great-grand-daughter of Mary Boleyn; the step-daughter of Robert Dudley, Earl of Leicester, Elizabeth I's long-time favourite; and the sister of Robert Devereux, Earl of Essex, Elizabeth I's last favourite.

Now, thanks to Sally Varlow's painstaking accumulation of detail, and engaging style, the charm, wit and beauty that made Lady Penelope the muse, not just of Sir Philip Sidney, but of poets, musicians and playwrights, leaps from the page, as does her warmth and generosity towards her family and friends.

Varlow also considers the relationship between Lady Penelope and her first husband, Lord Rich, more temperately than is often done. She shows that, for the early years of their marriage at least, the two got along as well as most partners in arranged marriages, and she also gives a plausible explanation of Rich's ongoing willingness to turn a blind eye to Lady Penelope's relationship with Lord Mountjoy.

One of the most interesting aspects of late sixteenth century life that the book illustrates, is the fluid nature of religious allegiance. Lady Penelope's grandfather, father, guardian, step-father and husband were all strong adherents of the Protestant, even Puritan cause, yet she herself flirted with Catholicism, apparently almost converting under the eloquence of Father John Gerard.

Unfortunately, the very charisma that Lady Penelope exerted in her own time, seems to have unduly influenced the author, too. The book crosses the line between a positive interpretation of the subject, and an almost novelistic identification with her.

Whilst I prefer biographers to at least like their protagonist, this should not render them completely blind to their flaws, nor should it cloud their judgement on the subject's interaction with the wider world. The author seems to struggle to understand that Elizabeth I had a duty beyond pandering to the sense of entitlement that seems to have permeated Penelope and Essex's whole life. Just because Essex wanted to be her chief minister, and Penelope wanted it for him, does not mean that Elizabeth should have placed him in that role. Varlow, however, gives the impression that this failure on Elizabeth's part to promote Essex to the level of his own view of himself, was a reflection of the Queen's 'corrupt' government.

One of Varlow's recurring theories, is that Elizabeth I favoured Lady Penelope, not just as the descendant of Elizabeth's aunt, Mary Boleyn, but because her grand-mother, Katherine, rather than being the daughter of Mary's husband, William Carey, was, in fact, the illegitimate daughter of Henry VIII. Whilst the evidence adduced by the author that Katherine Carey was Henry's daughter is certainly plausible, the argument is far from bearing from the *'almost-certain'* weight that she gives it. There is no evidence relating to the length of Henry VIII and Mary Boleyn's relationship – it may have gone on for several years, as Varlow contends. Equally, it might have been a brief fling. Further, to claim that Mary Boleyn would not have slept with her husband because she was having an affair with the King, cannot be more than speculation.

Overall, the book was enjoyable and informative, giving an interesting insight into the factional politics of the late Elizabethan age but, in my view, it would probably have been better as a novel.

Bibliography

Calendar of State Papers Simancas, British History Online (HMSO, 1892) Hume, Martin A S, ed.,

Calendar of State Papers: Venice <http://www.british-history.ac.uk/cal-state-papers/venice/vol2/vii-lxi> [accessed 7 October 2015]

Cecil Papers, http://www.british-history.ac.uk/cal-cecil-papers (Accessed: 7 September 2015)

Borman, Tracy, *Elizabeth's Women: The Hidden Story of the Virgin Queen*, Kindle (London: Jonathan Cape, 2009)

Butler, M. *The Court Masque*, The Cambridge Edition of the Works of Ben Johnson - Online Edition (2015)

Childs, Jessie, *God's Traitors: Terror and Faith in Elizabethan England* (United States: Oxford University Press, USA, 2014)

De Lisle, Leanda, *Tudor: The Family Story* (United Kingdom: Chatto & Windus, 2013)

Doran, S. *Elizabeth I and her Circle* 1st edn. (Oxford: OUP, 2015)

Doran, S. *The Tudor Chronicles.* (London: Quercus Publishing Plc, 2008)

Fletcher, A. and Vernon, L. (1973) *Tudor Rebellions (Seminar Studies in History).* 2nd edn. Harlow: Longman.

Lemon, Robert, ed., *Calendar of State Papers: Domestic Series: Edward, Mary and Elizabeth,* British History Online (London: HMSO, 1856)

Sidney, Philip, *'Jane the Quene': Being Some Account of the Life and Literary Remains of Lady Jane Dudley, Commonly Called Lady Jane Grey* (London: Swann, Sonneschein and Co., 1900)

Strickland, A. and Strickland, E. (2011) *Lives of the Queens of England from the Norman Conquest: Volume 3 & 4*. United Kingdom: Cambridge University Press (Virtual Publishing).

Varlow, S. *The Lady Penelope: The Lost Tale of Love and Politics in the Court of Elizabeth I* (London: Andre Deutsch. 2008)

Warnicke, R. M. *Wicked Women of Tudor England: Queens, Aristocrats, Commoners* (New York, NY: Palgrave Macmillan, 2012)

Weir, Alison, *Elizabeth, the Queen,* Kindle (London: Random House UK, 2009)

Whitelock, Anna, *Elizabeth's Bedfellows*, Kindle (London: Bloomsbury Publishing plc, 2013)

Woudhuysen, H. R. *Philip Sidney and the Circulation of Manuscripts, 1558-1640* (New York: Oxford University Press, 1996)

Durant, David N. *Bess of Hardwick: Portrait of an Elizabethan Dynast*, 1st edn (London: Distributed in the USA by Dufour Editions, 1999)

Footer, Donald *Women's Works: 900 - 1550*, 1st edn (New York: Wicked Good Books, 2013)

Fraser, William, *The Douglas Book*, 4 vols. (Edinburgh, 1885)

Leslie, John, The History of Scotland: From the Death of King James I, in the Year 1436 to 1561 (United States: Kessinger Publishing, 2007)

Shulman, Nicola, *Graven with Diamonds: The Many Lives of Thomas Wyatt: Courtier, Poet, Assassin, Spy* (London: Short Books, 2011)

Weir, Alison, *The Lost Tudor Princess* (London: Jonathan Cape 2015)

www.ingramcontent.com/pod-product-compliance
Lightning Source LLC
Chambersburg PA
CBHW030312030426
42337CB00012B/680